How the World Really Works
INSURANCE AT LLOYD'S OF LONDON

Published by Guy Fox History Project Limited
Illustrated by Students at Christchurch Primary School, Brick Lane, London

How the World Really Works:
Insurance at Lloyd's of London

Guy Fox History Project Limited

FIFTH EDITION

Copyright © 2024 Guy Fox History Project Limited

www.guyfox.org.uk

All rights reserved. No part of this publication may be reproduced, photocopied, stored in a retrieval system, or transmitted in any form or by any means, electronic, mechanical or otherwise, without the prior permission of Guy Fox History Project Limited.

This book was illustrated with assistance from students at
Christchurch Primary School whose drawings are used with their kind permission.

Originally funded by Lloyd's of London and supported by volunteers from the Lloyd's market. This edition was made possible thanks to support from readers like YOU!

Printed and bound in Great Britain

Contents

Introduction 4

PART ONE: INSURANCE 7

The Origins of Insurance 7

How Insurance Works 17

Types of Insurance 26

How an Insurance Company Makes a Profit 31

PART TWO: LLOYD'S OF LONDON 44

The History of Lloyd's of London 46

How Lloyd's of London Works Today 52

A Visit to the Lloyd's Building 65

Insurance Words 72

About the Project 76

Introduction

This book will tell you ALL about Insurance and how it REALLY works.

In Part One, this book will tell you about Insurance: how it started, how it works, and how Insurance Companies make money.

At the end of this book, you'll find a glossary of Insurance Words; it includes all the words marked in PURPLE in the book.

A few words to get you started:

Risk is the possibility that something bad might happen.

Loss is when something happens which leaves you worse off than you were before.

Insurance is a service which protects against loss.

PART ONE: INSURANCE
The Origins of Insurance

On the night of 2nd September 1666, a fire started in Pudding Lane. Soon it was out of control.

It burned for 4 days. There was no fire brigade, so people watched as the whole City went up in smoke. They called it the 'Great Fire of London'.

Finally, King Charles II sent the army to put it out.
But the Great Fire of London had destroyed:

13,500 houses,
87 churches,
and 44 livery halls,
plus
the Customs House,
the Royal Exchange and
the old St Paul's Cathedral.

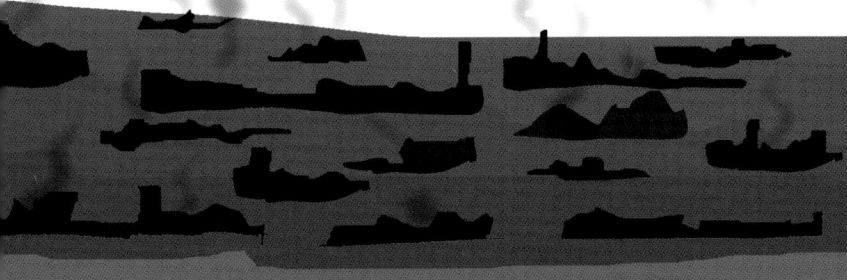

Nicholas Barbon had a good idea. He formed a company to protect buildings against the risk of fire.

Plus, Nicholas Barbon offered compensation so tha his customers could replace the things they lost.

It WAS a great idea, which spread to other countries. Insurance became a worldwide industry.

Since then, Insurance has grown into a huge industry. People buy Insurance to protect themselves in case of all sorts of loss.

How Insurance Works

① You have something which is at risk of loss.

② Your 'something' is at risk from various kinds of loss

③ So you contact an Insurance Company to see if they'll insure it. They'll ask you lots of questions:

④ The Insurance Company compares your answers to their statistics. This is information about car owners

⑤ If the Insurance Company accepts your risk, they check which coverage you'll need in case of loss.

⑥ After you decide your coverage, the Insurance Company asks you to pay a premium. They accept the risk and give you an Insurance Policy.

> The Insurance Policy is a contract.
>
> It tells you how much coverage you have and the expiration date for the Insurance.
>
> It also tells you about any exceptions to your Insurance!

⑦ That's it! You have peace of mind, knowing that your car is insured for a certain period of time.

> Insurance doesn't keep bad things from happening. But it does keep you from worrying about any loss!

But what if something bad does happen?

Here's What Happens When You Make an Insurance Claim:

You contact your Insurance Company and tell them what happened.

You tell them how much it will cost to fix or replace your car.

They might send around a claims adjustor to check your claim.

You may have to pay a bit of money towards the cost of fixing or replacing your car.
(This is called an excess.)

Once they accept your claim, they will pay to fix or replace your car.

Types of Insurance

LOTS of people have similar risks in life, so Insurance Companies offer popular types of Insurance for them

If there is a risk, and enough people need protection against it, there is probably a type of Insurance for it.

For example, LOTS of people need Travel Insurance to protect them in case of loss while they're on holiday.

Lots of people buy Home Insurance for their home (and the things inside) in case of fire or bad weather or theft.

Lots of people buy Pet Insurance for their dog or cat (or pet rabbit) in case it gets lost or needs medical treatment.

Of course, lots of people buy Car Insurance for their cars in case of fire or collision or theft.

Lots of people buy Bicycle Insurance for their bicycle in case of damage or theft.

Lots of people buy Health Insurance to protect themselves in case they need to pay big medical bills.

Lots of people buy Business Insurance, to protect their business in case something happens to the building, staff or equipment, or in case someone sues them.

These are a few popular types of Insurance which Insurance Companies offer. But there are more!

How an Insurance Company Makes a Profit

To make a profit, an Insurance Company needs LOTS of different customers!

Here's How It Works:

Let's say, an Insurance Company has 15,000 customers. Every customer pays a premium of £2,000 each year for Insurance.

15,000 customers × £2,000 = £30,000,000
(Yes, that's £30 million.)

The Insurance Company has a pool of £30 million to pay claims.

If 2,000 customers make a claim of £10,000 each: that's 2,000 × £10,000 = £20,000,000

So that's £30 million (in the pool)
minus £20 million in claims
minus operating costs (£5 million)
= A profit of £5 million.

Where in the world would you find Insurance to protect against the risks to your space satellite?

Or what if your company wants to protect its large cargo ships... or a fleet of airplanes?

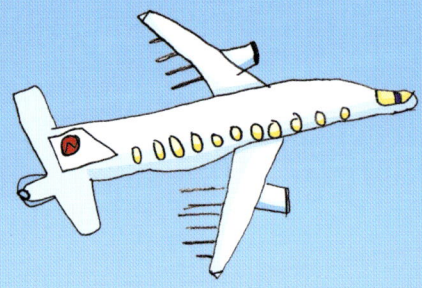

What if you're an explorer? Where would you find Insurance for your global balloon expedition?

Or maybe you're the boss of a huge company, and you want to insure your company against the unusual risks at your factory.

Or you're the boss of an energy company who wants to purchase Insurance for your windfarm.

Or what if you were a star footballer, and you wanted to protect your legs from the risk of injury?

You'd need a special Insurance Market full of experts who understand complicated and unusual risks.

You'd need... Lloyd's of London!

PART TWO: LLOYD'S OF LONDON

The History of Lloyd's of London

Lloyd's started in the 17th century in a coffee house near the River Thames.

Back then, there was a new craze: COFFEE!

Rich merchants would sit in coffee houses all day, drinking coffee and conducting their business.

f he decided to accept the risk, the merchant would WRITE his name on the slip, UNDER the details.

The merchants called their activities 'underwriting'. Every year, more and more ship owners came to Lloyd's Coffee House to arrange their Insurance.

The underwriting activities outgrew the coffee house, so the merchants set up a special market for Marine Insurance.

How Lloyd's of London Works Today

We're going to tell you about each role, but first, let us present the most important role of all:

Policyholder (the customer!)

> My company needs special Insurance for our drilling equipment!

He discusses his company's risk with a broker.
The broker asks A LOT of questions.
She needs to understand the risk.

The broker writes up the risk on an underwriting slip and discusses it with an underwriter at Lloyd's.

If the underwriter decides to accept the risk, he signs the underwriting slip and asks for a premium.

The first underwriter may accept only part of the risk. So the broker discusses it with another underwriter... and then another... until all of the risk has been accepted.

Managing Agents Are VERY Busy!

They employ the underwriters and organise their underwriting activities.

They try to make sure the underwriters charge enough premium for the risk, or else the syndicate will run out of money!

They employ people who handle claims made by their policyholders.

And they employ people who keep track of all the premiums and payments.

Managing agents charge the members of their syndicate a management fee.

They also get part of the syndicate's profit.

The world has changed a lot since Edward Lloyd's day, and so have the risks! The people who work in the Insurance Market at Lloyd's are always looking for creative ways to respond to new risks!

If Edward Lloyd came back for a visit today, I wonder what he would think?

A Visit to the Lloyd's Building

Lord Richard Rogers designed the Lloyd's Building. Here's what he said about it:

> Lloyd's began 350 years ago as a coffee shop; now, its headquarters building has been nicknamed 'The Espresso Machine'!

During your visit, you'll see many things which honour the history and innovation of Lloyd's.

When you visit Lloyd's, you'll see the Underwriting Room where brokers meet with underwriters.

In the Underwriting Room, you'll see a history exhibit, including Admiral Lord Nelson's special fork

You'll also see the 'loss book' which lists ships that have been lost at sea...

Take the glass lift to the 11th floor, and you'll find the Adam Room. It's a room from the 18th century! It is used for special meetings and dinners.

The Lloyd's Building also includes office space and meeting rooms and the usual things you'd expect.

THE END

Insurance Words

Bicycle Insurance
popular Insurance which protects you against the loss of your bicycle

Business Insurance
popular Insurance which protects you against losses to your business

Broker
a 'middle man' between the customer and the Insurance Company

Car Insurance
popular Insurance which protects you against the loss of your car

Central Fund
a pool of money at Lloyd's that can be used to pay claims to protect policyholders

Claim
request which a policyholder makes to their Insurance Company after a loss

Claims Adjustor
an agent who verifies Insurance claims

Class
a specialty area of underwriting

Collision
a crash or accident

Compensation
a payment given for a service or to make things right

Contract
a legal agreement

Corporate Member
a company which is a member at Lloyd's of London

Corporation of Lloyd's
the official name of the organisation which is called "Lloyd's of London"

Coverage
details of the losses your Insurance protects and at which financial value

Damage
when something is made worse

Energy Insurance
a class of Insurance underwritten at Lloyd's for energy company risks

Exceptions
the things which are NOT covered by an Insurance Policy

Excess
an amount the customer pays towards the loss; also known as a 'deductible'

Experts
people who have special knowledge or experience in a given field

Expiration
the date your Insurance Policy finishes

Health Insurance
popular Insurance which protects you against loss in case of poor health

Home Insurance
popular Insurance which protects you against the loss of your home or the things inside it

Innovation
thinking up ideas for better ways to do things

Insurable
an adjective describing something that can be insured; things which have only sentimental value cannot be insured

Insurance
a form of protection against loss

Insurance Market
a place where Insurance Companies sell Insurance

Insurance Policy
complete details of your Insurance

Invests
to make an investment; an investment is the use of money in the hope that it will make more money

Loss
when something happens which leaves you worse off than you were before

Lloyd's of London
a unique Insurance Market where underwriters create Insurance Policies for unusual or complicated risks

Managing Agent
the company who employs the underwriters and takes care of the syndicates at Lloyd's of London

Marine Insurance
a class of Insurance underwritten at Lloyd's for risks associated with ships and other sea-going vessels

Member
the person or company who pays claims if there isn't enough money in the syndicate's premium pool

Merchants
those who buy and sell goods and services in order to make a profit

Name
a person who is a member at Lloyd's of London

Pet Insurance
popular Insurance which protects you against loss in case your pet requires medical treatment

Policyholder
the person or company that buys an Insurance Policy; the customer!

Pool
a large amount of money

Possible
an adjective which describes a future event which may or may not happen

Premium
the amount of money the customer pays for an Insurance Policy

Profit
the amount of money a company makes, minus the amount of money it spends

Property Insurance
a class of Insurance underwritten at Lloyd's for risks associated with buildings

Reinsurance
a class of Insurance underwritten at Lloyd's for risks associated with Insurance

Risk
possibility that something bad might happen

Statistics
information which helps an Insurance Company to decide how likely a loss is for a policyholder

Syndicate
A group of members at Lloyd's of London which are looked after by managing agents

Term
the period of time during which your Insurance is valid

Thatched
a roof made from dried straw, water reed, sedge, rushes and heather

Theft
the act of stealing something that doesn't belong to you

Travel Insurance
popular Insurance which protects you against loss during your holiday

Underwriter
an expert who considers an unusual risk and decides whether or not to accept it

Underwriting
accepting a risk by writing your name at the bottom of the underwriting slip

Underwriting Room
a special room in the Lloyd's Building where brokers meet with underwriters

Underwriting Slip
the details of the unusual or complicated risk; also called the 'slip'

Unique
one-of-a-kind

Further Resources:
To learn more about Insurance and Lloyd's of London, try these websites:

Association of British Insurers
www.abi.org.uk

Lloyd's of London
www.lloyds.com

For information about 'How the World REALLY Works' and other projects visit:
www.guyfox.org.uk

About the Project

How the World Really Works **INSURANCE AT LLOYD'S OF LONDON** was developed in a collaboration among volunteers from the Lloyd's market, the Guy Fox team and students from Christchurch Primary School, Brick Lane, London. Students explored the world of Insurance, visited the Lloyd's building in the City of London and created the illustrations for this guide.

Illustrators: Abdal, Adnan, Dawit, Farhana, Khadeja, Momota, Nadia, Nathan, Niha, Ridwan, Sabina, Samme, Shabana, Shazia, Tanya, Tanzim and William

With Thanks to: Angela Dunlop, Martin Leach, Helen Ashenden, Karen Fairhurst, Alex Sarafoglou, Amee Shah, Christalla Andrews, Joyce Royle, Sandy Yates, Shahnara Begum, Reg Brown, Kiran Bhovan, George Doughty, Philip Godwin, William Armitage, Kirat Nandra, Olga Rakhmanina, Uli Farnes, Brendan Monaghan, Barry Maher, Paivi Autio, Pam Goodman, Shanan Wong-A-Fa, Rebecca Blinkhorn, Lyndsey Payne, Andy Sparrow, Kim Swan, Vicky Mirfin, Natalie Tickle, Nick Furlonge, Helena Yeaman, Sam James, Stuart Wilson, Carol Rider, Julian James, Alan Brown, Jenny Stephens, Giles Taylor, Jack Kent, Jamie Kilduff and the late Lord Richard Rogers

Guy Fox Staff & Volunteers: Eleanor Sanderson, Catherine Drennan, Oliver Boosey, Athanasia Arapogianni Konisti, Piera Lizzeri, Simon J. Harper, Mark Green, Kim Swan, Scott Unwin, Lana Kamffer and Kourtney Harper